Cover and Book Design by Brittany Bacinski
Follow Brittany on Instagram @brittanybacinski
Follow Amber on Instagram @mishkadawn

Published by All Good Juju, 2020

All Good Juju

Hippie Eats.

Family Cookbook

With Bonus Hippie Kids & Eco-Kitchen Sections Inside

**HIGH-VIBE, GLUTEN-FREE, SOY-FREE,
REFINED-SUGAR-FREE & VEGAN FRIENDLY
FLAVORFUL DISHES**

**By: Brittany Bacinski
& Amber Fokken**

Welcome to our table.

We're happy to feed you! It turns out our first and original Hippie Eats cookbook left folks craving even more. We're back and better than ever with brand new creations from the Hippie Kitchen.

Kick off your shoes, cozy up and get ready to cook the best-tasting, health-conscious meals that'll fool your family and friends into thinking they are as sinful as their old-time favorites.

brittany & amber

healthy noms
from 2 hippie moms.

We made this book for you. But first, we made it for our families. We wanted a place, a book if you will, to keep our favorite recipes.

When anyone is sick or looking for a healthier alternative to old classics, we still get texts asking, "Hey Britt, what's that vegan soup recipe?" or "Hey Amber, how can I eat more plant-based?"

Whatever it is, we've got the recipes our loved ones love in this very book. And that's pretty special.

All recipes are original health-forward family favorites. These are meals we eat regularly. We've learned over the years how to prepare healthy, plant-heavy meals without sacrificing flavor. We hope you love these meals as much as we do.

Enjoy!
Peace, love & plants,
Brittany & Amber

Table of Contents.

DESSERT

RECIPES

BANANA NUT PROTEIN MUFFINS

INGREDIENTS

- 2 cups all-purpose gluten-free flour
- 1 ½ tsp baking powder
- 1 tsp cinnamon
- ½ tsp baking soda
- ½ tsp salt
- ¼ tsp ground nutmeg
- 1 ¼ cups walnuts – chopped
- 1 scoop Protea vegan vanilla protein powder
- 3 overripe bananas – peeled and mashed
- 1 cup coconut sugar
- 8 tbsp vegan soy-free butter – melted & cooled
- 2 large eggs OR 2 vegan egg replacements, such as flax eggs
- ¼ cup plant milk
- 1 tsp vanilla extract

PREP TIME: 10 MINUTES
COOK TIME: 25 MINUTES
TOTAL TIME: 35 MINUTES

DIRECTIONS

1. Preheat oven to 350 degrees F. Spray a 12-count muffin pan with nonstick spray or use muffin liners. Set aside.
2. Prepare the dry ingredients: In a medium bowl, whisk together the flour, baking powder, ¾ teaspoon cinnamon, protein powder, baking soda, salt and nutmeg. Set aside.
3. Prepare the wet ingredients: In a large bowl with a handheld mixer, or in the bowl of a stand mixer fitted with wire whisk, beat the bananas with the sugar on medium speed until well whipped, about 2 minutes.
4. Add in the melted butter, eggs, milk and vanilla extract. Beat well, stopping to scrape down the sides of the bowl as needed.
5. Add the dry ingredients to the wet batter and use a rubber spatula to gently fold until everything is mostly combined. Add in the remaining ¾ cup walnuts and fold until all the ingredient are just combined – take care not to over-mix or the muffins will come out dry and dense.
6. Spoon the batter into the muffin tins, filling each tin ¾ of the way full. Sprinkle walnuts (and coarse sugar if using) evenly on top.
7. Bake at 350 degrees for 20-25 minutes or until golden brown and toothpick comes clean.
8. Allow the muffins to cool in the muffin pan for 5 minutes and then transfer them to a wire rack to cool completely.
9. Serve and enjoy!

INSIDE OUT MONKEY BREAD

INGREDIENTS

- 3 spotty medium-sized mashed bananas
- 2 whole eggs or flax egg subs
- 1/2 cup of coconut sugar
- 1/2 cup natural creamy nut butter (PB, almond butter, cashew or sunflower seed butter work, too)
- 1 tsp vanilla extract
- 1 1/4 cups flour (we used 1 cup of tiger nut flour and about 2 tbs of coconut flour)
- 1 tsp baking powder
- 1/2 tsp baking soda
- 1/4 tsp salt
- 1/4 cup vegan chocolate chips
- 2 tbsp cacao nibs, optional for the top

DIRECTIONS

1. In a medium bowl, combine all dry ingredients. Preheat oven to 350 degrees F.
2. In a large bowl, combine all the wet and dry ingredients. Mix using a large spoon, but do NOT over mix.
3. Use parchment paper to line bread pan. To make "swirly," set aside 1/3 of batter. Add 2 tbs of liquid oil of choice (avocado oil or coconut oil or butter substitute melted). Mix in 2 tbs of cacao powder and fold in 2-3 tbs of vegan chocolate chips, depending on how sweet you want it. Spoon in some of the larger mixture and then swirl in the chocolate mixture every few layers.
4. Bake for 55-60 minutes or until toothpick comes clean.
5. Serve warm and enjoy!

PREP TIME: 10 MINUTES
COOK TIME: 60 MINUTES
TOTAL TIME: 70 MINUTES

CHOCOLATE DESSERT HUMMUS

INGREDIENTS

- 1 can of organic chickpeas
- 1 tsbp cacao
- 1 tsbp of cocoa powder
- 1 tsp vanilla extract
- pinch of salt
- 1/3 cup of maple syrup
- 1 tbsp coconut sugar

DIRECTIONS

1. Add ingredients to a food processor or high powered blender.
2. Blend until smooth, scraping the sides as needed. Be patient! It usually takes a while for the chickpeas to break down and make a smooth consistency. It's worth the wait!
3. Transfer to a jar and store in the fridge for up to a week.
4. Enjoy on toast, in desserts, dipped with fruit or eat it "straight up!"

PREP TIME: 5 MINUTES
COOK TIME: 10 MINUTES
TOTAL TIME: 15 MINUTES

PUMPKIN SPICE DONUTS

INGREDIENTS

- 1/3 cup pumpkin puree
- 1/3 cup maple syrup
- 1 cup gluten-free oat flour
- 1 tsp baking powder
- 1/2 tsp baking soda
- 1/2 tsp cinnamon
- 1 tsp vanilla extract
- 1 tsp avocado oil
- 1 flax egg or 1 egg
- 1/2 cup plant milk
- 1 tsp pumpkin pie spice

DIRECTIONS

1. Combine dry ingredients into a mixing bowl. Preheat oven to 350 degrees.
2. Place wet ingredients into mixing bowl and mix until batter is smooth. Mix in pumpkin puree gently.
3. Place batter into donut pan (I found mine online), filling each donut 1/2 way to prevent overflowing.
4. Bake for 10 minutes or until toothpick comes clean.
5. Allow donuts to cool before serving. Makes 6 donuts.

PREP TIME: 10 MINUTES
COOK TIME: 15-20 MINUTES
TOTAL TIME: 25-30 MINUTES

LEMON COOKIE GRANOLA BUTTER

INGREDIENTS

- 1 1/3 cups gluten-free rolled oats
- 1/4 cup coconut oil- melted
- 2 tbsp maple syrup
- 2 tbsp coconut sugar
- 2 tsp lemon extract
- 1/2 tsp vanilla extract
- juice from half.a lemon
- 1/2 tsp pink himilayan salt

DIRECTIONS

1. Add ingredients to a food processor or high-powered blender.
2. Blend until smooth, scraping the sides as needed. Be patient! It usually takes a while for the oils to break down and make a butter consistency. It's worth the wait!
3. Transfer to a jar and store in the fridge for up to a week.
4. Enjoy on toast, in desserts, dipped with fruit or eat it "straight up!"

PREP TIME: 5 MINUTES
COOK TIME: 10 MINUTES
TOTAL TIME: 15 MINUTES

CHOCOLATE PROTEIN MOUSSE

INGREDIENTS

- 1 small container of unsweetened vegan vanilla yogurt or 1/2 cup
- 1 scoop of vegan chocolate protein powder
- optional: garnish with fresh fruit, cereal or granola

DIRECTIONS

1. In a bowl, mix together the yogurt and the scoop of protein powder until lumps are gone and the texture is smooth and whipped.
2. Garnish with garnish with fresh fruit, granola, cereal or granola.
3. Serve and enjoy!

PREP TIME: 5 MINUTES
COOK TIME: 0 MINUTES
TOTAL TIME: 5 MINUTES

PUMPKIN SPICE GRANOLA

INGREDIENTS

- 4 cups rolled gluten-free oats
- 1/4 cup vegan butter flavored coconut oil or vegan soy-free butter
- 1/3 unsweetened pumpkin puree
- 2 tsp ground cinnamon
- 2 tsp pumpkin spice
- 1/4 cup avocado oil
- 2 tbsp vanilla extract
- 1 cup of maple syrup
- 2 tbsp chia seeds
- 2 tbsp hemp seeds
- 1 tsp pink himalayan sea salt

DIRECTIONS

1. Combine wet and dry ingredients into a large mixing bowl.
2. Preheat oven to 300 degrees.
3. Gently toss granola mix until coated evenly with oil and spices.
4. Place onto baking sheet, spreading evenly to remove clumps and bake evenly. If you prefer chunky granola, don't worry about spreading out the mix too thin.
5. Bake for 10 minutes, then mix ingredients with spatula to ensure an even bake, then bake again for another 10 minutes or until golden brown.
6. Remove baking sheet and allow granola mix to cool for up to 1 hour or so. The granola will be crunchier over the time it cools. Lightly dust pink salt over the granola as it's cooling.
7. Enjoy granola over yogurt, fruit, with milk as a homemade cereal or eat it plain!

PREP TIME: 10 MINUTES
COOK TIME: 20 MINUTES
TOTAL TIME: 30 MINUTES

CHOCOLATE CHIP VEGAN PIZOOKIE

INGREDIENTS

- 1/2 cup white rice flour, oat flour or almond flour- all work
- 1 flax egg or 1 egg
- 1/3 cup coconut sugar
- 1/4 cup melted vegan butter
- 1/4 tsp baking soda
- 1/4 tsp salt
- 1/2 cup vegan semi-sweet chocolate chips
- 1 tsp vanilla extract

PREP TIME: 10 MINUTES
COOK TIME: 20 MINUTES
TOTAL TIME: 30 MINUTES

DIRECTIONS

1. Preheat your oven to 350°F and generously oil or butter a 6 1/4" mini cast iron skillet. If you don't have such a skillet, you could use a 6' cake pan instead, but you may have to adjust baking time slightly. You may also try doubling the recipe for a larger cast iron skillet as well.
2. Combine the flour, baking soda and salt in a bowl and mix well with a whisk until well combined; set aside.
3. In a separate mixing bowl, combine the sugar and vanilla extract. Add the melted butter and stir with a fork until well-combined. Add the egg (flax egg or regular), stir well, and then carefully stir in the flour mixture.
4. Mix until completely combined, then stir about 2/3 of the chocolate chips.
5. Transfer the cookie dough to the cast iron skillet, and arrange it delicately with your fork, just so it's evenly distributed across the skillet.
6. Bake for about 18-20 minutes, or until the edges are puffed and browned and the center appears set.

GRANNY'S APPLE CRISP

INGREDIENTS

- 6 peeled apples
- 1/2 cup coconut sugar
- 2 cups gluten-free rolled oats
- 1/2 gluten-free oat flour
- pinch of salt
- 6 tbsp melted soy-free vegan butter
- 2 1/2 tsp cinnamon, ground

DIRECTIONS

1. Preheat oven to 350 degrees.
2. In a medium mixing bowl, combine sugar, butter and cinnamon. Stir until well-combined.
3. Add the sliced apples and stir until all apples are well coated.
4. Pour apple mixture into 9×13 baking dish. In a separate bowl add flour, oats, coconut sugar and cinnamon.
5. Sprinkle it over the apple mixture and bake for 35-40 minutes or until golden brown.
6. Let it cool slightly, and enjoy right away!

PREP TIME: 10 MINUTES
COOK TIME: 35-40 MINUTES
TOTAL TIME: 50 MINUTES

PUMPKIN SPICE COOKIES WITH VEGAN CREAM CHEESE FROSTING

INGREDIENTS

- 1/2 cup vegan soy-free butter, softened
- 3/4 cup coconut sugar
- 3/4 cup maple syrup
- 1 1/4 cups canned pumpkin
- 1 tsp pure vanilla extract
- 2 cups oat flour or all purpose gluten-free flour
- 1 flax egg
- 1/2 cup almond flour
- 1 tsp baking soda
- 1 tsp baking powder
- 1 tbsp cinnamon
- 2 tsp pumpkin pie spice
- 1/2 tsp salt

For the frosting:
- 1/2 cup soy-free vegan butter, softened
- 3 cups powdered sugar
- 2 tbsp vegan cream cheese
- 1/2 tsp vanilla extract
- 1-2 tbsp plant milk, as needed to thin

PREP TIME: 10 MINUTES
COOK TIME: 20 MINUTES
TOTAL TIME: 30 MINUTES

DIRECTIONS

1. Preheat the oven to 350 degrees and line a baking sheet with parchment paper.
2. In a large bowl, cream together the vegan butter with both the maple syrup and coconut sugar. You can use a hand mixer or even a large wooden spoon if needed.
3. Mix in 1 1/4 cups canned pumpkin and vanilla until well-combined and smooth.
4. Add the flour to the bowl, and sprinkle the baking soda, baking powder, cinnamon, ginger and salt on top of the flour. Stir until well-combined and a dough is formed. The dough will be sticky.
5. Place heaping tablespoons (about 1 1/2-2 tbsp) on the prepared baking sheet. Flatten the cookie with your palms to keep a cookie shape. The dough will be sticky, so wet your hands before pressing down.
6. Bake for 11-14 minutes.
7. Remove from the oven and let them sit on the baking sheet for 5 minutes before transferring to a cooling rack.
8. Make the frosting: Using a hand mixer mix frosting ingredients. Once the cookies have cooled completely, frost generously and sprinkle with a little bit of cinnamon. Enjoy!

DOUBLE CHOCOLATE VEGAN MUFFINS

INGREDIENTS

- 1 1/2 spotty bananas
- 2 cups gluten-free oat flour
- 1 tbsp cocoa powder
- 1/4 cup vegan chocolate chips
- 1 tbsp sunflower seed butter or almond butter
- 1 1/3 cup milk
- 1 tsp baking soda
- 1/2 tsp baking powder
- 1 flax egg
- pinch of salt
- 1 tsp vanilla extract

DIRECTIONS

1. Preheat oven to 350 degrees. Combine wet and dry ingredients into mixing bowl.
2. Mix batter evenly. With ice cream scoop, scoop out batter in a muffin pan.
3. Place muffin pan in oven and cook for 25 minutes or until tops are golden and a toothpick comes out clean.
4. Let cool before serving.

PREP TIME: 10 MINUTES
COOK TIME: 25 MINUTES
TOTAL TIME: 35 MINUTES

VEGAN SUGAR COOKIES

INGREDIENTS

- 3 cups all-purpose gluten-free flour
- 1/2 tsp almond extract
- 1 tsp baking powder
- 1/2 tsp baking soda
- 1 tsp natural vegan food coloring (we use Supernatural brand)
- 3 cups vegan powdered sugar, for frosting
- 1/2 tsp salt
- 2 tsp vanilla extract, for dough
- 1 tsp vanilla extract, for frosting
- 1/2 cup soy-free vegan butter, for frosting
- 1 1/2 cups coconut sugar
- 1 1/3 cup plant milk
- 1 tbsp lemon juice
- 1 3/4 cups vegan butter, for dough

PREP TIME: 20 MINUTES
COOK TIME: 15 MINUTES
TOTAL TIME: 35 MINUTES

DIRECTIONS

1. Preheat oven to 350 degrees. Line two large baking sheets with parchment paper. In a medium bowl whisk together the dry ingredients. In a large bowl, use a stand mixer or hand mixer to beat the vegan butter and sugar together until fluffy.
2. Add the remaining wet ingredients and combine. The mixture won't combine well and will look curdled and that's totally fine.
3. Then, add the dry ingredients into the bowl with the wet, and mix together. The dough will be very soft, feel free to chill for 1 hour before scooping to make it easier.
4. Next, scoop 2 tablespoons of cookie dough and drop it onto the parchment paper lined baking sheet. Repeat to fill your pan, evenly spacing the cookies. Wet your fingers so they don't stick to the cookies, then lightly pat the balls down into flatter shapes.
5. Bake 11 - 14 minutes until lightly golden on the bottom. Let cool completely before frosting.
6. To make the frosting: using a hand mixer, beat together the vegan butter, powdered sugar, and vanilla extract. If needed add 1 tablespoon of plant milk at a time until desired frosting consistency is reached. Mix in food color if desired.
7. To assemble the cookies: spread frosting on the cooled cookies then decorate with sprinkles if desired. Enjoy!

SALTED DATE CARAMEL

INGREDIENTS

- 1/2 can full fat
- 1/4 tsp pink salt
- 1/4 cup of maple syrup
- 1 tsp vanilla extract
- 1 1/2 cup pitted dates

DIRECTIONS

1. Add dates to a high speed blender along with salt, maple syrup, vanilla and coconut milk to a food processor or high-powered blender.
2. Blend until smooth, scraping the sides as needed.
3. Transfer to a jar and store in the fridge for up to a week.
4. Enjoy in drinks, desserts and eat it "straight up!"

PREP TIME: 10 MINUTES
COOK TIME: 0 MINUTES
TOTAL TIME: 10 MINUTES

VEGAN MARSHMALLOW FLUFF

INGREDIENTS

- 1 part aquafaba, which is the the juice from the can of chickpeas. Sounds gross but it's neutral in taste!
- 1 tsp lemon juice (I used this instead of cream of tartar)
- 1 tsp almond extract
- 1 tsp vanilla extract
- 2 tbsp maple syrup (honey works too)
- 2 tbsp arrowroot powder
- 1/2 cup organic vegan powered sugar

DIRECTIONS

1. We used 1 part aquafaba, which is the the juice from the can of chickpeas. Sounds gross but it's neutral in taste!
2. Add to a large mixing bowl and whip together a 1 tsp lemon juice, 1 tsp almond extract, 1 tsp vanilla extract, 2 tbsp maple syrup (honey works, too), 2 tbsp arrowroot powder, and 1/2 cup organic powered sugar in a large bowl with a hand mixer or stand mixer for 6 minutes.
3. Whip until light and fluffy. Serve and enjoy!

PREP TIME: 10 MINUTES
COOK TIME: 6 MINUTES
TOTAL TIME: 16 MINUTES

VEGAN MARSHMALLOW CRISPY TREATS

INGREDIENTS

- 10 ounces vegan marshmallows (large bag of vegan marshmallows) or to make a homemade marshmallow like the photo above, use our homemade marshmallow whip recipe on the previous page, but also mix together 2 tsp agar agar powder or 3 tbsp grass fed gelatin if not vegan with 6 tbsp of water in a separate pot, heat until it's a warm liquid. Add this to the marshmallow whip in a large bowl and beat for 1 minute. Quickly place the mixture into a silicone ice cube tray that is dusted with arrow root powder. Slice the edges off with an index card or knife and dust again with arrow root powder. Let sit for 20 minutes, pop out and enjoy! You made a homemade marshmallow! Go you!)
- 1/4 cup soy-free vegan butter
- 4 2/3 cups gluten-free vegan crispy rice cereal

DIRECTIONS

1. Grease an 8-inch or 9-inch square pan with coconut oil or vegan butter. Cut the large marshmallows into 4 small pieces and place them in a saucepan. Add the vegan butter and set over low heat.
2. Heat, stirring often until softened and somewhat melted. Use the back of a rubber spatula or a wooden spoon to smash the marshmallows until they break down.
3. Stir in the crispy rice cereal. Then use your hands, cautiously as the marshmallows are hot, to fully combine the cereal and marshmallows together.
4. Gently press the cereal mixture into an 8-inch or 9-inch square pan.
5. Allow the treats to cool for at least 30 minutes before cutting into rectangles or squares. Serve and enjoy!

PREP TIME: 10 MINUTES
COOK TIME: 5 MINUTES

VEGAN SMORES COOKIE BARS

INGREDIENTS

- 1/2 cup melted soy-free vegan butter
- 3/4 cup coconut sugar
- 1 tsp pure vanilla extract
- 3 tablespoons plant milk
- 1 3/4 cups all purpose flour
- 1/2 tsp baking powder
- 1/4 tsp salt
- 1 1/4 cups vegan chocolate chip chips
- 1 package of vegan marshmallows
- For drizzle: 2 tbsp coconut oil melted with 4 tbsp of vegan chocolate chips

DIRECTIONS

1. Preheat oven at 350 for 12 minutes in a small 8x8 square pan.
2. Spray pan with non-stick oil.
3. In a large bowl, whisk together the melted vegan butter, coconut sugar, vanilla and plant milk until smooth.Next, add the flour, baking powder and salt and mix until combined. Add the cookie dough mixture into the pan and push it down evenly with your hands.
4. Bake for 15 minutes until golden brown. Then add the marshmallows on top and bake for another 10-15 minutes. May also broil for just a couple of minutes to make the marshmallows even more toasty, but watch closely, so it doesn't burn!
5. Let cool for 10 minutes and drizzle with melted vegan chocolate. Slice and serve. Enjoy!

PREP TIME: 10 MINUTES
COOK TIME: 25 MINUTES
TOTAL TIME: 35 MINUTES

VEGAN CRANBERRY MUFFINS

INGREDIENTS

- 2 cups gluten-free all purpose flour
- 1 cup oat milk
- 1 tsp vanilla
- pinch salt
- 1/3 cup maple syrup
- 1 1/2 cup frozen or fresh cranberries
- 2 tsp baking powder
- 1/4 tsp cinnamon
- 1/2 cup apple sauce
- 2 tbsp avocado oil
- optional: add chopped walnuts to batter

DIRECTIONS

1. a medium bowl, combine all dry ingredients. Preheat oven to 350 degrees F.
2. Spray a cupcake/muffin pan with coconut oil spray.
3. In a large bowl, combine all the wet and dry ingredients. Mix using a large spoon, but do NOT over mix.
4. Using an ice-cream scoop or spoon, scoop the batter into each cupcake holder.
5. Bake for 25-30 minutes, or until toothpick comes clean. Makes 12 muffins.
6. Serve warm and enjoy!

PREP TIME: 10 MINUTES
COOK TIME: 30 MINUTES
TOTAL TIME: 40 MINUTES

VEGAN CHOCOLATE PUDDING PIE

INGREDIENTS

- 1/2 can coconut cream
- 1/2 cup coconut sugar
- 4 tbsp arrowroot powder
- 1/3 cup melted vegan chocolate chips
- 1 tbsp avocado oil (to mix with chocolate)
- 3 tbsp cocoa powder
- 2 tbsp oat milk creamer
- 1 pre-made gluten-free, soy-free, vegan pie crust OR feel free to make your own
- coconut whipped cream, to garnish

DIRECTIONS

1. In a small bowl, mix oat milk creamer and arrowroot powder with a whisk and set aside. In a medium saucepan, whisk together canned coconut cream and sugar then heat on medium high until just boiling.
2. Reduce to low then stir in chocolate chips, avocado oil and cocoa powder. Let cook while whisking until smooth. Increase heat to medium and slowly add arrowroot mixture into the pan while still whisking. Let cook until the mixture is thick, like pudding (5 minutes).
3. Remove from heat and if necessary, add pudding mixture to bowl and use a hand mixer to make smooth and pourable.
4. Assemble the pie: pour filling into cooled crust. Let pie cool completely or chill in the refrigerator for 8 hours (or overnight). Top with coconut whipped cream.

PREP TIME: 10 MINUTES
COOK TIME: 15 MINUTES
TOTAL TIME: 25 MINUTES

SAVORY

RECIPES

VEGAN ZUCCHINI FRITTER WITH SRIACHA DILL SAUCE

INGREDIENTS

- 4 cups shredded zucchini, about 1 pound
- 3/4 cup gluten-free oat flour
- 1/4 cup nutritional yeast
- 1/4 cup olive oil
- 1 tsp baking powder
- 1 tsp gsrlic powder
- 2 tbsp vegan parmesan, optional
- 2 tbsp oil, for cookingsalt and pepper, to taste

Dipping sauce
- 3 tbsp soy-free vegan mayo
- 1 tsp sriacha
- 1/3 tsp lemon juice
- 1/4 dill

DIRECTIONS

1. In a food processor or blender with your shredder attachment, shred the zucchini. You also can use a handheld shredder instead. Using a cheesecloth or thin kitchen towel, squeeze any excess liquid out of the zucchini.
2. Transfer the zucchini into a large bowl, and add the remaining ingredients EXCEPT the cooking oil.
3. Mix together until you have a uniform batter. Taste and adjust seasoning. Heat oil over medium heat in a large nonstick sauté pan.
4. Once the oil is hot, scoop fritter batter, 1/4 cup at a time, onto the hot oil and flatten into a fritter that is about 3" around. Sauté for 3-4 minutes per side until edges are crispy brown and the zucchini is cooked all the way through.
5. Repeat until all the batter is used.
6. Serve immediately with siracha dill sauce.

PREP TIME: 10 MINUTES
COOK TIME: 20 MINUTES
TOTAL TIME: 30 MINUTES

CHEEZY VEGGIE & POTATO BAKE

INGREDIENTS

- 5 golden potaotes, cubed
- 1 zucchini, chopped
- 1/2 white onion, diced
- 1 red bell pepper, diced
- 1 tsp garlic powder
- 2 tbsp avocado oil
- salt and pepper to taste
- 1 cup vegan cheddar style cheese

DIRECTIONS

1. In a medium bowl, combine potatoes, veggies and spices. Evenly coat with avocado oil. Preheat oven to 350 degrees F.
3. In a baking dish, place potato and veggie mixture inside with a layer of vegan cheddar style cheese on top.
4. Bake for 35-40 minutes, or until potatoes are soft.
5. Serve warm and enjoy! Add tofu, beans, vegan meat or regular meat if you wish.

PREP TIME: 10 MINUTES
COOK TIME: 35 MINUTES
TOTAL TIME: 45 MINUTES

THE MISHKA VEGGIE SANDWHICH

INGREDIENTS

- 2 slices of GF vegan bread, a simple sourdough is best
- 1 tsp mustard
- 1 tbsp vegan mayo
- 2 slices of tomato
- 1 handful of spinach or romaine
- 2 chopped broccoli florets
- 2 slices of avocado
- 4 slices of thinly-cut cucumber
- 1 slice of vegan cheese

DIRECTIONS

1. Start with layering the condiments on to the bread.
2. Add cheese, romaine/spinach, avocado and other veggies.
3. Sandwich all ingredients together between your bread. Slice, serve and enjoy!

PREP TIME: 5 MINUTES
COOK TIME: 0 MINUTES
TOTAL TIME: 5 MINUTES

TURMERIC LEMON VEGGIE DETOX SOUP

INGREDIENTS

- 1 container of vegetable broth
- 1 tsp turmeric powder
- 1 lemon, juiced
- 1/2 small white onion, chopped
- 5 medium golden potatoes, cubed
- 1 cup cherry tomatoes or 1 can of diced tomatoes
- 5 carrots chopped
- 2 cups of broccoli
- 1 cup of peas
- 1 cup of chopped celery
- 2 cloves of garlic, chopped finely
- salt and pepper to taste

DIRECTIONS

1. Chop the onion and sauté it until soft in a medium-sized saucepan.
2. Cut the potatoes into cubes and add them to the pan, along with the broth, lemon juice, turmeric and spices.
3. Bring to a boil. Then, simmer covered for about 15 minutes.
4. Stir over low heat until veggies and potatoes are soft.
5. Enjoy warm!

PREP TIME: 5 MINUTES
COOK TIME: 35 MINUTES
TOTAL TIME: 40 MINUTES

HOMEMADE TOMATO BASIL SPAGHETTI SAUCE

INGREDIENTS

- 1/4 cup basil, fresh
- 2 bay leaves
- 4 cloves garlic, chopped
- 1 tbsp oregano, dried
- 1 28- ounce can San marzano tomatoes
- 1 tsp nutritional yeast
- 1 white onion, chopped
- 1/2 tsp black pepper
- 1 tbsp coconut sugar
- 1 pinch red pepper flakes
- 3/4 tsp salt

1.1 tbsp olive oil

DIRECTIONS

1. Heat olive oil in a 5-quart Dutch oven or soup pot.
2. Add onion and sauté until translucent and soft; about 4 minutes.
3. Add minced garlic, oregano, red pepper flakes and bay leaves. Stir and cook for 1 minute. Stir in crushed tomatoes, tomato sauce, tomato paste, chicken broth, sugar, vinegar and fresh chopped basil.
4. Bring to a boil, cover, and reduce heat to low. Simmer for at least 30 minutes to an hour, stirring occasionally.
5. Meanwhile, cook spaghetti (or your favorite pasta) according to package directions. Drain (do not rinse) and toss with homemade spaghetti sauce. Garnish with fresh basil leaves, if desired.
6. Enjoy!

PREP TIME: 10 MINUTES
COOK TIME: 60 MINUTES
TOTAL TIME: 70 MINUTES

WHITE CHICKEN CHILI

INGREDIENTS

- 2 containers of veggie broth
- 1/2 can full fat coconut milk
- 3-4 chicken breasts shredded or 3-4 cups shredded jack fruit
- 1/2 jar mild salsa
- 1 red onion, diced
- 1/3 cup green onion, chopped
- 6 peeled poatoes, cubed
- 1/2 lime, juiced
- 1 can pinto beans, drained
- 1 can great northern beans, drained
- 2 jalapenos (or 1 can mild green chiles)
- 1 tbsp ground cumin
- 2 tsp chili powder
- salt and pepper to taste
- 1/3 cup fresh, chopped cilantro optional but recommended

For garnish:
- tortilla strips or chips
- extra cilantro or chopped green onion
- avocado slices
- extra lime wedge

PREP TIME: 30 MINUTES
COOK TIME: 30 MINUTES
TOTAL TIME: 60 MINUTES

DIRECTIONS

1. Boil and shred chicken. Set aside.
2. In a separate pot, cook potatoes until soft but not mushy. Set aside.
3. In a large stew pot, add the coconut milk, broth, onion, veggies and spices. Bring to a boil and reduce to a simmer.
4. Simmer until veggies are soft. Add spices, chicken and potatoes to the pot.
5. Garnish and serve immediately.

VEGAN CREAMY BROCCOLI AND LEMON PASTA

INGREDIENTS

- 1 lemon, squeezed
- 1/2 can full fat coconut milk
- 4 tbsp nutritional yeast
- 2 tbsp soy-free vegan butter or vegan butter flavor coconut oil, melted
- 2 cups broccoli, fresh or frozen
- 1 tsp garlic powder
- salt and pepper to taste (bonus if you have lemon pepper seasoning)
- salt and pepper to taste
- 1 box of high protein chickpea pasta (or brown rice noodles work, too!)

DIRECTIONS

1. Boil water and cook pasta. Once pasta is cooked, drain and set aside.
2. To make the sauce, add lemon juice, garlic, coconut milk. sea salt, and nutritional yeast in a blender.
3. Blend on high until creamy and smooth.
4. Place broccoli in a rimmed skillet with the butter and cook until broccoli is wilted and mushrooms are softer.
5. Add sauce to the skillet with the vegetables and heat over medium-low heat, stirring frequently until sauce is hot and slightly thickened.
6. To serve, add cooked pasta to the sauce and toss to combine. Serve warm!

PREP TIME: 10 MINUTES
COOK TIME: 35 MINUTES
TOTAL TIME: 45 MINUTES

EASY CHEEZY QUESADILLA

INGREDIENTS

- 2 tortillas
- 3/4 cup vegan cheese shreds
- 1/4 cup smashed pinto beans
- 1/4 cup bell peppers, chopped
- 2 tbsp onions, chopped
- handful of spinach
- salsa of choice for dipping

DIRECTIONS

1. Heat nonstick pan over medium-low heat and spray oil.
2. Place one tortilla on top of the oil. On one half of the tortilla, sprinkle half the cheese. On top of the cheese, arrange half the beans, half the peppers, half the onions. Sprinkle more cheese, if you like.
3. Gently, fold one side of the tortilla to the other side in half. Cook one side until it's golden brown. Reduce heat, if necessary to prevent burning.
4. Then, gently flip it and cook the other side until golden brown.
5. Remove from pan and let it sit for 1 minute and then cut it in half and serve with salsa. Repeat those steps with the other tortilla. Enjoy!

PREP TIME: 5 MINUTES
COOK TIME: 0 MINUTES
TOTAL TIME: 5 MINUTES

SIMPLE AND FRESH GUACAMOLE

INGREDIENTS

- 3 medium avocados
- ½ tsp garlic powder
- ½ tsp onion powder or 1/4 fresh red onion, diced
- salt to taste
- pepper to taste
- 2 tbsp lime juice
- 2 tbsp chopped fresh cilantro
- 2 small tomatoes diced
- a dash of hot sauce, optional but recommended
- fresh cilantro recommeded

DIRECTIONS

1. Cut open avocados lengthwise, remove the pit, and use a spoon to scoop out the flesh into a medium-sized mixing bowl. Use a potato masher or fork and gently mash the avocado, leaving it a little bit chunky at this point.
2. Add garlic powder, onion powder, salt, pepper, hot sauce and lime juice.
3. If you would like your guacamole smoother, use a fork or your potato masher to mix in the spices as you mash the mixture. If you like your guacamole a little chunkier, use a rubber spatula to stir in the spices until well-combined!
4. Add cilantro, onions and tomatoes and stir until combined. Taste and add extra salt or lime juice if needed! Serve with plantain chips for a low calorie, low fat, grain-free and healthy snack!

PREP TIME: 5 MINUTES
COOK TIME: 0 MINUTES
TOTAL TIME: 5 MINUTES

BUFFALO VEGAN RANCH DIP

INGREDIENTS

- 1 cup plain unsweetened coconut milk yogurt (any plain unsweetened vegan yogurt will work as long as it is tart in flavor)
- 2 tbsp tahini
- 1 lemon, juiced
- 1/4 tsp garlic powder
- 1/4 tsp onion powder
- 1/4 dill, fresh or dried
- 2 tbsp hot wings sauce or hot sauce will work

DIRECTIONS

1. In a medium bowl, combine all ingredients and whisk until smooth.
2. Serve with carrots, celery or use a salad dressing.
3. Enjoy!

PREP TIME: 7 MINUTES
COOK TIME: 0 MINUTES
TOTAL TIME: 7 MINUTES

PAN FRIED CABBAGE & POTATOES

INGREDIENTS

- 1 package shredded green cabbage (5 cups)
- 3 russet potatoes, peeled and chopped
- 1/4 white onion, diced
- 1 sweet potatoes peeled and chopped
- 1/2 red bell pepper, diced
- 1/2 green bell pepper, diced
- 2 cloves garlic, minced
- salt and pepper to taste
- 1 tbsp olive oil

DIRECTIONS

1. Add potatoes, cabbage, salt, and pepper to the pan, stirring with olive oil.
2. Cover with a lid and cook until potatoes and cabbage are tender, removing the lid to occasionally stir.
3. Add minced garlic to the pan, stirring with other ingredients until fragrant, about a minute. Remove the pan from heat. Add a protein of choice if you wish.

REP TIME: 10 MINUTES
OOK TIME: 25MINUTES
OTAL TIME: 35 MINUTES

QUARANTINE QUICK BREAD

INGREDIENTS

- 1/2 cup of oat flour (almond flour works, too)
- 2 tbsp olive oil
- 1/4 cup vegan parmesan cheese shreds OR 2 tbsp nutritional yeast
- 1 tbsp Italian spices (oregano, basil, garlic powder, and onion powder)
- 1 tbsp of water
- 1/2 tsp of pink salt

DIRECTIONS

1. In a medium bowl, combine all ingredients.
2. Preheat oven to 350 degrees F.
3. Mix dough evenly with hands. It will be sticky,but feel free to add a little water as needed. Careful not to add too much water, the dough shouldn't be runny.
4. Roll dough into a ball onto parchment paper, then flatten using a rolling pin.
5. Once dough is flat, place onto a pan and bake for 15 minutes or until edges are slightly golden. Feel free to add more vegan cheese to the top to make a cheesy style garlic bread.
6. Serve warm!

PREP TIME: 10 MINUTES
COOK TIME: 15 MINUTES
TOTAL TIME: 25 MINUTES

VEGAN VEGGIE CREAM CHEEZE PIZZA

INGREDIENTS

- 1/2 cup of oat flour (almond flour works, too)
- 2 tbsp olive oil
- 1/4 cup vegan parmeason cheese shreds OR 2 tbsp nutrtional yeast
- 1 tbsp italian spices (oregano, basil, garlic powder, and onion powder)
- 1 tbsp of water
- 1/2 tsp of pink salt
- 1 container of vegan cream cheese (we used an almond chive cream cheese)
- 1/4 cup chopped broccoli
- 1/4 cup chopped carrot
- 1/4 cup chopped cherry tomato

DIRECTIONS

1. In a medium bowl, combine all ingredients except the chopped veggies and vegan cream cheese.
2. Preheat oven to 350 degrees F.
3. Mix dough evenly with hands. It will be sticky,but feel free to add a little water as needed. Careful not to add too much water, the dough shouldn't be runny.
4. Roll dough into a ball onto parchment paper, then flatten using a rolling pin.
5. Once dough is flat, place onto a pan and bake for 15 minutes or until edges are slightly golden.
6. Let dough cool completely. Spread the cream cheese over the dough entirely.
7. Layer veggies on top to complete your veggie pizza.
6. Slice like pizza and serve immediately. Enjoy!

PREP TIME: 10 MINUTES
COOK TIME: 15 MINUTES
TOTAL TIME: 25 MINUTES

VEGAN PHO

INGREDIENTS

- 1 container of veggie broth (chicken broth works well, too)
- 1 package of gluten-free millet brown rice ramen-style noodles
- 2 cloves of minced garlic (or 1 tsp garlic powder)
- 1/2 tsp ginger
- dash of clove
- 2 tbsp coconut aminos
- 1/2 tsp coconut sugar or date sugar
- 1 tsp onion powder
- 1 cup of mushrooms
- salt and pepper to taste
- red pepper flakes or cayenne to taste
- 1/2 sliced jalapeno
- 1/2 diced yellow onion
- 1 cup thin carrot ribbons
- 1/2 cup mushrooms
- garnish: cilantro, jalapeño

PREP TIME: 5 MINUTES
COOK TIME: 15 MINUTES
TOTAL TIME: 20 MINUTES

DIRECTIONS

1. Place noodles into medium pot with the broth.
2. Bring noodles to a boil. Add in spices, garlic and veggies to the broth. (Any veggies work or you can keep it simply broth and noodles.)
3. Simmer until noodles are done and soft.
4. Garnish and enjoy served warm!

VEGAN SHEPHERD'S PIE

INGREDIENTS

- 1 cup brown lentils or green lentils, canned lentils work too
- 3-4 cups vegetable broth
- 2 tsp olive oil
- ½ cup onion, chopped
- 1 cup chopped mushrooms a
- 1 carrot peeled and chopped
- 1 rib celery, chopped
- ½ cup frozen peas, defrosted
- 3 tbsp red wine
- 2 tsp coconut aminos
- 3 tbsp tomato paste
- 1/2 tsp garlic powder
- 2 tbsp parsley, fresh or dried
- salt and pepper to taste
- 2 ½ cups prepared mashed potatoes (mash together potatoes with plant milk and 2 tbsp soy-free vegan butter)

DIRECTIONS

1. Preheat oven to 400°F.
2. Combine lentils and 3 cups broth in a saucepan and bring to a boil. Reduce heat to a simmer and cover. 3. 3. Cook for 20-25 minutes or until lentils are tender. Meanwhile, cook onion, mushrooms, carrot, and celery in olive oil over medium heat until onion and carrot are softened.
4. Add lentils (and their broth), red wine, coconut aminos and tomato paste. Stir in peas and simmer uncovered 10 minutes, adding more broth as needed to create a sauce. Stir in parsley and seasonings.
5. Spoon lentil mixture into a deep-dish pie plate. Top with mashed potatoes and bake 20-25 minutes or until potatoes are browned.
6. Serve warm and enjoy!

PREP TIME: 10 MINUTES
COOK TIME: 20-25 MINUTES
TOTAL TIME: 30-35 MINUTES

LAZY MOM 2 INGREDIENT TOMATO SOUP

INGREDIENTS

- 1/2 jar of all-natural tomato marina sauce (best current brand is Raos Homemade)
- 1 cup unsweetned plant milk
- add additonal italian seaonings if you'd like

DIRECTIONS

1. In a medium pot, pour milk and marina sauce. Bring to a simmer. Add additonal seasonings if you'd like.
2. Serve warm and enjoy!

PREP TIME: 2 MINUTES
COOK TIME: 10 MINUTES
TOTAL TIME: 12 MINUTES

VEGAN BUTTER ROSEMARY BISQUITS

INGREDIENTS

- 2 cups unsweetened plant milk +(1 tbsp apple cider vinegar)
- 4 cups all purpose gluten-free flour, plus more as needed for rolling (you can try with a grain-free flour such as cassava or almond flour, but we haven't tested it!)
- 2 tbsp baking powder
- 1/2 tsp baking soda
- 1 1/2 tsp pink salt
- 1 tsp coconut sugar
- 1 tsp fresh or dried rosemary

PREP TIME: 30 MINUTES
COOK TIME: 12 MINUTES
TOTAL TIME: 42 MINUTES

DIRECTIONS

1. Preheat the oven to 425 degrees F.
2. Stir the apple cider vinegar into the non-dairy milk; this is called your buttermilk. Then, place in the freezer for 30 minutes to get very cold. Don't skip this step!
3. As soon as the "buttermilk" is in the freezer, melt the vegan butter in the microwave. Let cool at room temperature.
4. Once vegan butter is melted, whisk together dry ingredients. Place the bowl in the freezer.
5. When your timer goes off, remove the "buttermilk" from the freezer. Stir the icy bits into the "buttermilk", then drizzle the melted and cooled vegan butter into the very cold milk, one large spoonful at a time. Spoon milk over the drizzled butter but do not stir in the butter, you want clumps of butter to form in the cold milk.
6. Whisk the 4 cups flour, almond flour, baking powder, baking soda and salt in a large bowl.
7. Add the milk/vinegar mixture into the dry ingredients, and mix. Avoid overstirring.
8. Place dough onto a floured surface and work it in your hands, adding a little more flour if it's too sticky.
9. Roll the dough about 1/2 inch thick, then use a biscuit cutter or a drinking glass to cut out the biscuit circles.
10. Continue re-rolling the dough until you have used it all. Place the biscuits on a baking sheet lined with a silicone mat or parchment paper.
11. Bake for about 12 minutes until light golden brown and fluffy. Allow to cool for a few minutes, serve and enjoy!

HEALTHIER SLOPPY JOES

INGREDIENTS

- 2 tsp garlic powder
- 1 cup cooked or canned lentils, meat alternative of choices
- 1/2 yellow onion, chopped
- 1 tbsp coconut aminos
- 1 15-ounce can tomato sauce
- 1 tsp chili powder
- 2 tbsp yellow mustard
- 1 tbsp coconut sugar
- 1 pinch paprika, smoked or regular
- salt and pepper to taste
- 2 tbsp avocado oil
- 1 package of hamburger buns, gluten-free or vegan bread of choice

DIRECTIONS

1. First, cook the lentils or protein of choice. You may also use canned lentils.
2. Heat a large skillet over medium heat. Once hot, add the chopped onion and oil. Cook until onions are translucent. Now add the spices, coconut aminos, mustard, coconut sugar and stir for about 1 minute. Add a little water if it's too dry. Season with salt to taste.
3. Serve on burger buns and enjoy!

PREP TIME: 5 MINUTES
COOK TIME: 20 MINUTES
TOTAL TIME: 25 MINUTES

SPANISH STYLE SAUSAGE PAELLA

INGREDIENTS

- 2 heaping tbsp soy-free butter or vegan butter flavored coconut oil
- 1 cup of Raos Homemade Marinara Sauce (This sauce is the best, it's not cheap but the flavor is worth it. You may also sub with a homemade red sauce or another brand)
- 1 1/2 cup of frozen peas
- 1/2 white onion, diced
- 2 cups of jasmine or basmati rice, cooked
- 1/4 tsp paprika
- 1/4 tsp garlic powder
- 1 tsp chili powder
- 1/4 tsp cayenne pepper or omit if you don't like it spicy
- 1 container veggie broth (to cook rice in instead of water)
- 2 cups of cooked/ sauteed chicken sausage (vegan sausage works!) or shredded chicken is great, too (or use shredded jackfruit to make vegan "shredded chicken")
- salt and pepper to taste

DIRECTIONS

1. Sautee sausage until cooked (or boil and shred chicken) and set aside.
2. In a separate pot, cook basmati rice in veggie broth for extra flavor until done. Set aside.
3. In a large pan or dutch oven pan, add butter, peas and onion. Cook until onion is translucent. Turn heat down to medium before adding in other ingredients.
4. Add cooked rice into the veggie mix. Add spices, red sauce and either chicken or sausage as well. Slowly stir until sauce and spices evenly cover the rice. Adjust seasonings to taste, feel free to add more red sauce if you feel it needs it.
5. Serve immediately. Enjoy!

PREP TIME: 30 MINUTES
COOK TIME: 30 MINUTES
TOTAL TIME: 60 MINUTES

JUICING

RECIPES

IMMUNITY JUICE

INGREDIENTS

- 1/4 pineapple, juiced
- 3 oranges, juiced
- 1 small 1 inch knob of ginger, juiced
- 2 small nuggets of turmeric, juiced
- pinch of black pepper

DIRECTIONS

1. Wash produce thoroughly. Always chop any ends, stems and remove any large seeds or pits. Slice oranges away from their peel. Citrus peels are extremely bitter when juiced. Slice again to make produce small enough to fit through a juicer.
2. Push produce and any chopped slices through a high powered slow masticating juicer.
3. Stir juices together, add pepper at the end and serve.
4. Drink immediately for full benefits, otherwise store in a sealed container in the fridge for up to 3 days.

EARTH GARDEN JUICE

INGREDIENTS

- 1 whole bunch of celery
- 4 oranges, peeled
- 1 lemon, peeled
- 3 carrots
- 1 cucumber, peeled

DIRECTIONS

1. Wash produce thoroughly. Always chop any ends, stems and remove any large seeds or pits.
2. Push produce and any chopped slices through a high powered slow masticating juicer.
3. Stir juices together and serve.
4. Drink immediately for full benefits, otherwise store in a sealed container in the fridge for up to 3 days.

GRAPE LEMON JUICE

INGREDIENTS

- 1 whole bag of green grapes
- 2 lemons, sliced away from peel

DIRECTIONS

1. Wash produce thoroughly. Always chop any ends, stems and remove any large seeds or pits.
2. Push produce and any chopped slices through a high powered slow masticating juicer.
3. Stir juices together and serve.
4. Drink immediately for full benefits otherwise, store in a sealed container in the fridge for up to 3 days.

SWEET DEEP GREENS JUICE

INGREDIENTS

- 2 oranges
- 3 green apples
- 1 lemon
- 1 whole stalk of celery
- 5 leafs of kale
- 1 peeled cucumber

DIRECTIONS

1. Wash produce thoroughly. Always chop any ends, stems and remove any large seeds or pits. Slice and chop apple away from its core and lemon and oranges away from its peel. Citrus peels are very bitter when juiced. Chop celery from its base.
2. Push produce and any chopped slices through a high powered slow masticating juicer.
3. Stir juices together and serve.
4. Drink immediately for full benefits, otherwise store in a sealed container in the fridge for up to 3 days.

SWEETER THAN CANDY JUICE

INGREDIENTS

- 3 peeled sweet potatoes
- 6 carrots
- 3 peeled oranges
- 4 red apples

DIRECTIONS

1. Wash produce thoroughly. Always chop any ends, stems and remove any large seeds or pits.
2. Push produce and any chopped slices through a high powered slow masticating juicer.
3. Stir juices together and serve.
4. Drink immediately for full benefits, otherwise store in a sealed container in the fridge for up to 3 days.

CRANBERRY APPLE PEAR GINGER JUICE

INGREDIENTS

- 3 apples
- 4 pears
- 1 cup fresh cranberries
- 1 knob of ginger

DIRECTIONS

1. Wash produce thoroughly. Always chop any ends, stems and remove any large seeds or pits.
2. Push produce and any chopped slices through a high powered slow masticating juicer.
3. Stir juices together and serve.
4. Drink immediately for full benefits, otherwise store in a sealed container in the fridge for up to 3 days.

JAY'S FAVE JUICE

INGREDIENTS

- 6 apples
- 1 whole bunch of celery
- 1 lemon
- 1 inch, small knob of ginger

DIRECTIONS

1. Wash produce thoroughly. Always chop any ends, stems and remove any large seeds or pits.
2. Push produce and any chopped slices through a high powered slow masticating juicer.
3. Stir juices together and serve.
4. Drink immediately for full benefits, otherwise store in a sealed container in the fridge for up to 3 days.

ENERGIZING RED JUICE

INGREDIENTS

- 1/2 of a beet
- 1 lemon
- 6 apples
- 4 carrots

DIRECTIONS

1. Wash produce thoroughly. Always chop any ends, stems and remove any large seeds or pits. Slice and chop apple away from its core and lemon away from its peel. Citrus peels are very bitter when juiced. Chop beet away from the root.
2. Push produce and any chopped slices through a high powered slow masticating juicer.
3. Stir juices together and serve.
4. Drink immediately for full benefits, otherwise store in a sealed container in the fridge for up to 3 days.

G.I JANE JUICE (FOR YOUR GUT)

INGREDIENTS

- 1/2 head of cabbage
- 1 lemon, peeled
- 5 pineapple spears
- 3 apples
- 1 large peeled cucumber

DIRECTIONS

1. Wash produce thoroughly. Always chop any ends, stems and remove any large seeds or pits.
2. Push produce and any chopped slices through a high powered slow masticating juicer.
3. Stir juices together and serve.
4. Drink immediately for full benefits, otherwise store in a sealed container in the fridge for up to 3 days.

WATERMELON LIME JUICE

INGREDIENTS

- 1/2 watermelon
- 2 limes
- for extra hydration add a sprinkle of pink himalayan salt

DIRECTIONS

1. Wash produce thoroughly. Always chop any ends, stems and remove any large seeds or pits.
2. Push produce and any chopped slices through a high powered slow masticating juicer.
3. Stir juices together and serve.
4. Drink immediately for full benefits otherwise store in a sealed container in the fridge for up to 3 days

BUBBLICIOUS GUM JUICE

INGREDIENTS

- 1/4 of a whole peeled pineapple or about 6 spears
- 1/4 chopped watermelon
- 3 peeled cucumbers

DIRECTIONS

1. Wash produce thoroughly. Always chop any ends, stems and remove any large seeds or pits. Slice and chop pineapple and watermelon away from its rind. Slice again to make produce small enough to fit through a juicer.
2. Push produce and any chopped slices through a high powered slow masticating juicer.
3. Stir juices together and serve.
4. Drink immediately for full benefits otherwise, store in a sealed container in the fridge for up to 3 days.

NATURES FLU SUPPORT

INGREDIENTS

- 2 nuggets of turmeric
- 4 large oranges
- 4 large carrots
- pinch of black pepper

DIRECTIONS

1. Wash produce thoroughly. Always chop any ends, stems and remove any large seeds or pits.
2. Push produce and any chopped slices through a high powered slow masticating juicer.
3. Stir juices together and serve.
4. Drink immediately for full benefits, otherwise store in a sealed container in the fridge for up to 3 days.

LIQUID SUNSHINE JUICE

INGREDIENTS

- 6 apples
- 6 oranges
- 2 lemons
- 1 small 1 inch knob of ginger

DIRECTIONS

1. Wash produce thoroughly. Always chop any ends, stems and remove any large seeds or pits. Slice and chop apple away from its core and slice oranges and lemons away from its peel. Citrus peels are extremely bitter when juiced. Slice again to make produce small enough to fit through a juicer.
2. Push produce and any chopped slices through a high powered slow masticating juicer.
3. Stir juices together and serve.
4. Drink immediately for full benefits, otherwise store in a sealed container in the fridge for up to 3 days.

DETOX & HYDRATE

INGREDIENTS

- 1/3 watermelon
- 3 lemons
- 4 apples
- 1 knob of ginger
- for extra hydration, add a sprinkle of pink himalayan salt

DIRECTIONS

1. Wash produce thoroughly. Always chop any ends, stems and remove any large seeds or pits.
2. Push produce and any chopped slices through a high powered slow masticating juicer.
3. Stir juices together and serve.
4. Drink immediately for full benefits, otherwise store in a sealed container in the fridge for up to 3 days.

SWEET APPLE CARROT JUICE

INGREDIENTS

- 6 carrots
- 6 apples

DIRECTIONS

1. Wash produce thoroughly. Always chop any ends, stems and remove any large seeds or pits. Slice and chop apple away from its core.
2. Push produce and any chopped slices through a high powered slow masticating juicer.
3. Stir juices together and serve.
4. Drink immediately for full benefits, otherwise store in a sealed container in the fridge for up to 3 days.

SMOOTH AND REFRESHING GREEN JUICE

INGREDIENTS

- 6 ribs of celery
- 1 cucumber peeled
- 1 cup of spinach
- 4 red apples
- 2 pears
- 1 lime

DIRECTIONS

1. Wash produce thoroughly. Always chop any ends, stems and remove any large seeds or pits. Slice and chop apples away from its core. Slice lime away from its peel and chop in half.
2. Push produce and any chopped slices through a high powered slow masticating juicer.
3. Stir juices together and serve.
4. Drink immediately for full benefits, otherwise store in a sealed container in the fridge for up to 3 days.

TRIPPY ORANGE JUICE

INGREDIENTS

- 2 carrots
- 6 oranges
- 1 small 1 inch knob of ginger
- 4-5 pineapple spears

DIRECTIONS

1. Wash produce thoroughly. Always chop any ends, stems and remove any large seeds or pits. Slice and chop apples away from its core. Slice oranges and pineapple away from their peel and chop in half.
2. Push produce and any chopped slices through a high powered slow masticating juicer.
3. Stir juices together and serve.
4. Drink immediately for full benefits, otherwise store in a sealed container in the fridge for up to 3 days.

HYDRATING AND CLEANSING GREEN JUICE

INGREDIENTS

- 1/4 bunch of parsley
- 4 red apples
- 1 lemon
- 1/2 stalk of celery
- 2 cups of spinach
- 2 cups of romaine

DIRECTIONS

1. Wash produce thoroughly. Always chop any ends, stems and remove any large seeds or pits. Slice and chop apples away from its core.
2. Push produce and any chopped slices through a high powered slow masticating juicer.
3. Stir juices together and serve.
4. Drink immediately for full benefits, otherwise store in a sealed container in the fridge for up to 3 days.

SMOOTHIE & DRINK

RECIPES

TURMERIC BANANA PROTEIN SMOOTHIE

INGREDIENTS

- 1 banana
- 3 large Medjool dates, pitted
- 3 tbsp shelled hemp seeds
- 1 tbsp ginger root, grated
- 1/2 tsp ground turmeric
- 2 cups plant milk
- optional: 1 scoop vegan protein powder

DIRECTIONS

1. Combine ingredients together into a blender.
2. Blend on high until smooth.
3. Pour into your favorite smoothie cup.
4. Enjoy immediately!

PREP TIME: 5 MINUTES
COOK TIME: 0 MINUTES
TOTAL TIME: 5 MINUTES

MOCHA CHIP NICE CREAM BOWL

INGREDIENTS

- 4 frozen bananas
- 2 tbsp of organic instant coffee
- 1 tbsp cacao
- 1 tsp chocolate extract (vanilla works, too)
- pinch of salt
- 4 dates or 2 tbsp maple syrup
- optional: for a protein boost, 1 scoop of vegan chocolate protein powder

DIRECTIONS

1. Combine ingredients together into a blender.
2. Blend on high until smooth.
3. Pour into your favorite smoothie cup.
4. Enjoy immediately!

PREP TIME: 5 MINUTES
COOK TIME: 0 MINUTES
TOTAL TIME: 5 MINUTES

SUPER CHERRY BERRY SMOOTHIE

INGREDIENTS

- 1 banana
- 2 dates
- 1 cup strawberries
- 1 cup cherries
- 1 cup raspberries
- 2 cups plant milk

DIRECTIONS

1. Combine ingredients together into a blender.
2. Blend on high until smooth.
3. Pour into your favorite smoothie cup.
4. Enjoy immediately!

PREP TIME: 5 MINUTES
COOK TIME: 0 MINUTES
TOTAL TIME: 5 MINUTES

COCONUT GINGER MANGO SMOOTHIE

INGREDIENTS

- 2 frozen bananas
- 1 cup frozen mango
- 1 inch of fresh ginger
- 2 cups coconut milk
- 2 dates
- optional: 1 scoop vanilla vegan protein powder
- optional: coconut shreds as a garnish

DIRECTIONS

1. Combine ingredients together into a blender.
2. Blend on high until smooth.
3. Pour into your favorite smoothie cup.
4. Enjoy immediately!

PREP TIME: 5 MINUTES
COOK TIME: 0 MINUTES
TOTAL TIME: 5 MINUTES

FRUITY PEBBLE SMOOTHIE

INGREDIENTS

- 3 frozen bananas
- 2-3 large oranges, juiced or
  1/2 cup orange juice
- 2 cups frozen strawberries
- 1/2 lemon, squeezed
- 2 tbsp hemp seeds
- 1 small container of mango
  vegan yogurt (optional but
  recommended)

DIRECTIONS

1. Combine ingredients together into a blender.
2. Blend on high until smooth.
3. Pour into your favorite smoothie cup.
4. Enjoy immediately!

PREP TIME: 5 MINUTES
COOK TIME: 0 MINUTES
TOTAL TIME: 5 MINUTES

FROZEN CHERRY BANANA NICE CREAM BOWL

INGREDIENTS

- 3 frozen bananas
- 1 cup frozen cherries
- 1 cup plant milk of choice (add a pinch more if consistency gets too thick)
- optional: 1 scoop vanilla vegan protein

DIRECTIONS

1. Combine ingredients together into a blender.
2. Blend on high until smooth.
3. Pour into your favorite smoothie bowl and top with cherries.
4. Enjoy immediately!

PREP TIME: 5 MINUTES
COOK TIME: 0 MINUTES
TOTAL TIME: 5 MINUTES

SWEET PUMPKIN SMOOTHIE BOWL WITH PUMPKIN SPICE GRANOLA

INGREDIENTS

- 1 cup ice
- 3 frozen bananas
- 1 cup plant milk
- 1/4 cup pumpkin puree
- optional: 1 scoop of vegan vanilla protein
- 1/4 tsp cinnamon
- 1/4 tsp pumpkin spice

DIRECTIONS

1. Combine all ingredients into a blender, leaving a few berries aside to garnish.
2. Blend until smooth and creamy. Pour into bowl and top with garnish.
3. Enjoy immediately.

PREP TIME: 5 MINUTES
COOK TIME: 0 MINUTES
TOTAL TIME: 5 MINUTES

SWEET FROZEN BLUEBERRY SMOOTHIE

INGREDIENTS

- 2 frozen bananas
- 2 cups plant milk
- 2 dates
- 2 cups frozen blueberries

DIRECTIONS

1. Combine ingredients together into a blender.
2. Blend on high until smooth.
3. Pour into your favorite smoothie cup.
4. Enjoy immediately!

PREP TIME: 5 MINUTES
COOK TIME: 0 MINUTES
TOTAL TIME: 5 MINUTES

ORANGE CREAMSICLE ON ICE

INGREDIENTS

- 2 oranges, juiced
- 1 tsp vanilla extract
- 1 cup almond milk or coconut milk

DIRECTIONS

1. Juice two oranges or use 1/2 cup orange juice.
2. Mix vanilla extract with almond milk. Add ice and pour into cup.
3. Pour orange juice over almond milk and ice.
4. Serve immediately!

PREP TIME: 5 MINUTES
COOK TIME: 0 MINUTES
TOTAL TIME: 5 MINUTES

WHIPPED VEGAN MATCHA

INGREDIENTS

- 1 tbsp matcha
- 1 tbsp hot water
- 2 tbsp coconut sugar
- 1 tbsp aquafaba (yes, the liquid from a can of chickpeas! You can't taste it, I promise).
- optional: small handful of muddled raspberries

DIRECTIONS

1. In a medium bowl, mix all ingredients together with a hand mixer for 3-4 minutes until whipped and foamy consistency.

2. Pour whipped matcha over ice and almond milk.

3. Optional but yummy, toss a small handful of muddled raspberries and/or raspberry extract for extra flavor!

PREP TIME: 5
COOK TIME: 5 MINUTES
TOTAL TIME: 10 MINUTES

BLACK FOREST CAKE SMOOTHIE

INGREDIENTS

- 1 tsp cacao nibs
- 2 1/2 cups unsweetened almond milk
- 2 1/2 tbsp unsweetened cocoa powder
- 4 medjool dates, pitted
- 1 tbsp chia seeds
- 1-2 handfuls baby spinach
- 2 cups frozen pitted cherries
- 1 tsp cacao powder
- optional: 1 scoop of chocolate vegan protein powder
- optional: 2 tbsp of walnuts

DIRECTIONS

1. Place all ingredients into blender.
2. Blend until smooth and creamy.
3. Serve immediately.

PREP TIME: 5 MINUTES
COOK TIME: 0 MINUTES
TOTAL TIME: 5 MINUTES

SALTED CARAMEL LATTE

INGREDIENTS

- 8 ounces brewed organic coffee
- 1/2 cup oat milk
- 2 tbsp full fat coconut cream
- 4 tbsp date caramel
- 1/2 tsp vanilla
- pinch of pink salt
- 1 tsp maple syrup

DIRECTIONS

1. In a sauce pan, mix together oat milk, maple syrup, coconut cream and date caramel. Cook on medium heat on the stove top until warm.

2. Pour in cup and use a frother or blend for 1 minute to foam the milk.

3. Pour coffee into a large mug, add the foamy milk mixture on top. Drizzle with date caramel and enjoy!

PREP TIME: 5 MINUTES
COOK TIME: 5 MINUTES
TOTAL TIME: 10 MINUTES

ORIGINAL FROTHY OAT MILK LATTE

INGREDIENTS

- 8 ounces brewed organic coffee
- 1/2 cup oat milk
- 1 tsp maple syrup

DIRECTIONS

1. Pour coffee over ice and add oatmilk to desired shade. Stir in maple syrup.
2. Pour additonal oat milk in a cup and use a frother or blend for 1 minute to foam the milk.
3. Pour coffee into a large mug, add the foamy milk mixture on top. Enjoy!

PREP TIME: 5 MINUTES
COOK TIME: 5 MINUTES
TOTAL TIME: 10 MINUTES

PUMPKIN SPICE FROTHY OAT MILK LATTE

INGREDIENTS

- 8 ounces brewed organic coffee or an espresso works, too
- 1/2 cup cashew milk
- 1 tsp maple syrup or honey
- 1/4 tsp pumpkin spice

DIRECTIONS

1. Pour coffee over ice and add cashew milk to desired shade. Stir in maple syrup and spices.
2. Pour additonal cashew milk in a cup and use a frother or blend for 1 minute to foam the milk.
3. Pour coffee into a large mug, add the foamy milk mixture on top. Sprinkle with cinnamon. Enjoy!

PREP TIME: 5 MINUTES
COOK TIME: 5 MINUTES
TOTAL TIME: 10 MINUTES

Hippie
Eats.

For The KidS Table

CHOCOLATE PROTEIN SMOOTHIE BOWL

INGREDIENTS

- 4 frozen bananas
- 1 cup plant milk
- 1 scoop vegan chcocolate protein
- 3 dates

DIRECTIONS

1. Combine all ingredients into a blender.
2. Blend until smooth and creamy. Pour into bowl and top with garnish.
3. Enjoy immediately.

PREP TIME: 5 MINUTES
COOK TIME: 30 MINUTES
TOTAL TIME: 5 MINUTES

BANANA SPRINKLE NICE CREAM

INGREDIENTS

- 4 frozen bananas
- 1 cup plant milk (use a tiny bit more if you need to keep the blender moving, but careful not too add too much or it will be too watery)
- natural dye-free sprinkles

DIRECTIONS

1. Combine all ingredients into a blender, leaving a few berries aside to garnish.
2. Blend until smooth and creamy. Pour into bowl and top with garnish.
3. Enjoy immediately.

PREP TIME: 5 MINUTES
COOK TIME: 0 MINUTES
TOTAL TIME: 5 MINUTES

DOUBLE CHOCOLATE SUPERFOOD GRANOLA BARS

INGREDIENTS

- 1/4 cup maple syrup
- 1/4 cup coconut sugar
- 3 tbsp coconut oil or avocado oil
- 1 tsp cacao
- 1 tsp vanilla extract
- pinch salt
- 1 cup chocolate brown rice cereal
- 1 1/2 cup rolled oats
- 1/4 cup vegan chocolate chips
- 3 tbsp hemp seeds
- 3 tbsp chia seeds
- optional : 1 scoop vegan chocolate protein powder

DIRECTIONS

1. Place maple syrup, coconut sugar, oil, cacao, vanilla and salt in a pot.
2. Bring ingredients to a hot liquid, but not fully boiled.
3. In a large separate bowl, add dry ingredients: brown rice cereal, oats, chocolate chips, hemp seeds, chia seeds and protein powder if you wish to add it. Mix using a large spoon.
4. Using a spatula, add wet mixture into dry mixture, slowly coating evenly. Mixture will be sticky.
5. Pack granola bar mixture very tightly into a 8x8 pan with parchment paper.
6. Let cool for 1 hr in fridge and harden before slicing into bars.

PREP TIME: 15 MINUTES
COOK TIME: 60 MINUTES
TOTAL TIME: 75 MINUTES

HEALTHY BANANA BOATS WITH SUNBUTTER

INGREDIENTS

- 1-2 bananas sliced horizontaly into boats
- 2 tbsp sunbutter or nut butter of choice
- 2 tbsp raisins

DIRECTIONS

1. Slice bananas into horizontal boats.
2. Top with sunbutter or nut butter of choice.
3. Add raisins or vegan chocolate chips on top for a healthy sweet tooth snack. Enjoy!

PREP TIME: 5 MINUTES
COOK TIME: 0 MINUTES
TOTAL TIME: 5 MINUTES

PINEAPPLE LEMONADE POPSICLES

INGREDIENTS

- 1/2 pineapple, juiced or 2 cups of pineapple juice
- 1 lemon, juiced

DIRECTIONS

1. Place lemon and pineapple juice into a container with a spout.
2. Pour contents into silicone popsicle molds.
3. Freeze until solid. Best if frozen overnight.
4. Enjoy immediately!

PREP TIME: 5 MINUTES
COOK TIME: 0 MINUTES
TOTAL TIME: 5 MINUTES

EASTAN'S "APPLE CREAMY"

INGREDIENTS

- 1 cup frothed oatmilk
- 1 cup coldpressed apple juice

DIRECTIONS

1. Place oatmilk into a mug and mix well with a milk frother or blend in a high-powered blender.
2. Pour juice into a cup of choice. Layer the foamy oatmilk on top.
3. Add ice if you'd like and drink immediately!

EASTAN'S "WATERMELON CREAMY"

INGREDIENTS

- 2 cups chopped watermelon (frozen is best!)
- 2 cups oatmilk

DIRECTIONS

1. Place all ingredients in a high powered blender.
2. Blend until smooth and creamy.
3. Add ice if you wish and enjoy!

PLANT BASED KIDDO SNACK PLATE

INGREDIENTS

- chickpeas or any beans
- fresh fruit
- granola bar
- fresh veggies

DIRECTIONS

1. On a colorful plate (kids eat with their eyes, too!) , set out several different options for your child's snack.

2. Silicone baking cups make great snack holders and can be an easy way to add more color to a meal and make it more fun.

3. Be sure to chop and slice each food item accordingly for your child's age. If you're unsure, ask your pediatrician.

PREP TIME: 5 MINUTES
COOK TIME: 0 MINUTES
TOTAL TIME: 5 MINUTES

VEGAN GF BANANA BIRTHDAY CAKE

INGREDIENTS

- 1 1/2 cup gluten-free flour
- 1/2 cup butter/soft but not melted
- 1 cup oat milk
- 2 vegan eggs
- 1/2 cup maple syrup
- 1 tsp vanilla extract
- pinch of pink salt
- 1 ripe spotty banana
- 1 tsp baking powder
- 1/4 tsp baking soda
- 1 tbsp apple cider vinegar
- feel free to use a vegan store bought vanilla frosting or make your own with vegan butter and vegan powdered sugar

PREP TIME: 10 MINUTES
COOK TIME: 30-35 MINUTES
TOTAL TIME: 40-45 MINUTES

DIRECTIONS

1. Preheat oven to 350°F. Lightly grease two 6- inch cake pans. Sprinkle a little flour into each pan, then shake the pan around to evenly distribute the flour.
2. In a large bowl, add flour, sugar, baking soda, and salt. Whisk to combine. Add milk, oil, vinegar, mashed banana (mash banana separately with a hand mixer until smooth before adding to mix) and vanilla; whisk until just combined. Do not overmix; it's okay if there are some lumps.
3. Divide the batter evenly between the two pans.
4. Bake for 35 minutes, until a toothpick inserted into the center of the cake comes out clean.
5. Set pans aside for 10 minutes to cool, then remove cake from pan and place on a cooling rack (a trick: place a plate on top of the pan, flip it over so that the cake comes out on the plate, then flip the plate over onto the cooling rack).
6. When completely cool, decorate with frosting and sprinkles. Enjoy!

CHOCOLATE CHIP MUG CAKE

INGREDIENTS

- 2 tbsp plant milk
- 2 tbsp vegan chocolate chips (optional)
- 1/4 tsp cinnamon
- 1 tbsp avocado oil
- 1/4 tsp baking powder
- 1/4 tsp cinnamon
- 2 tbsp coconut sugar
- 1/4 cup oat flour
- 1 tsp vanilla extract
- pinch of salt

DIRECTIONS

1. Combine all ingredients in a mixing bowl and mix until batter is smooth.
2. Scoop batter into a mug or mini ceramic bowl.
3. Microwave for 2-3 minutes.
4. Let cool and use oven mitt before removing if the mug or bowl doesn't have a handle, the cake gets pretty hot. Enjoy warm.

PREP TIME: 5 MINUTES
COOK TIME: 2 MINUTES
TOTAL TIME: 7 MINUTES

VEGAN VANILLA SPRINKLE WHOOPIE PIES

INGREDIENTS

- 1 1/2 cups all purpose flour, gluten-free
- 2 tsp baking powder
- 1/4 tsp baking soda
- 1/4 + 1/8 tsp salt
- 2/3 cup coconut sugar
- 1/3 cup avocado oil
- 2/3 cup plant milk
- 2 tsp apple cider vinegar
- 1 1/2 tsp vanilla extract
- frosting: feel free to use store bought vegan vanilla or homeade buttercream with vegan butter and vegan powdered sugar
- optional: dye-free food coloring (we used Supernatural plant-based brand for both food coloring and sprinkles)

PREP TIME: 20 MINUTES
COOK TIME: 20 MINUTES
TOTAL TIME: 40 MINUTES

DIRECTIONS

1. Preheat oven to 375 degrees F. Into a medium bowl, combine coconut sugar, oil, plant milk, vanilla and vinegar with a whisk.
2. Next, add flour, baking powder, baking soda and salt to the sifter and sift the dry ingredients into the wet ingredients. Combine with a whisk.
3. Line a baking tray with parchment and using a 1 1/2 tablespoon cookie scoop, portion the batter onto trays leaving 2 inches of space in between for spreading.
4. Bake for 10-12 minutes.
5. Remove from the oven and let cool on the pan for 5 minutes before moving to a cooling rack. And then repeat the process with the remaining batter.
6. Fill with buttercream frosting!

HEALTHY APPLESAUCE DONUTS

INGREDIENTS

- 2 cups gluten-free oat flour
- 1/4 cup maple syrup
- 1 tsp apple cider vinegar
- 1 cup plant milk
- 1 tsp vanilla extract
- pinch sea salt
- 1 flax egg or 1 egg
- 1/3 cup apple sauce
- 1 tsp cinnamon
- 2 tsp baking powder

DIRECTIONS

1. In a medium bowl, combine all dry ingredients.
2. Preheat oven to 350 degrees F.
3. Spray a donut pan with coconut oil spray.
4. In a large bowl, combine all the wet and dry ingredients. Mix using a large spoon, but do NOT over mix.
5. Using a spoon, scoop the batter into each cupcake holder.
6. Bake for 15 minutes or until toothpick comes clean.
7. Serve warm and enjoy!

PREP TIME: 10 MINUTES
COOK TIME: 15 MINUTES
TOTAL TIME: 25 MINUTES

10 MINUTE SNEAKY VEGGIE/FRUIT TOT COOKIES

INGREDIENTS

- 2 cups gluten-free oat flour
- 1/3 cup gluten-free oats (you can also use a package of instant GF oats)
- 1/4 cup maple syrup
- 1 baby food fruit/veggie pouch or 1/2 cup of pureed baby food of choice
- 1 tsp vanilla extract
- pinch sea salt
- 1 flax egg or 1 egg
- 1 tbsp hemp seeds
- 1/3 cup apple sauce
- 1 tsp cinnamon
- 2 tsp baking powder

DIRECTIONS

1. In a medium bowl, combine all ingredients. Preheat oven to 350 degrees F.
2. Spray cookie sheet pan with coconut oil spray.
3. Using a spoon, scoop the batter onto cookie sheet.
4. Bake for 15 minutes or until toothpick comes clean.
5. Serve warm and enjoy!

PREP TIME: 5 MINUTES
COOK TIME: 10 MINUTES
TOTAL TIME: 15 MINUTES

GARLIC BUTTER AND BROCCOLI NOODLES WITH SNEAKY PROTEIN

INGREDIENTS

- 2 tbsp soy-free vegan butter or vegan butter flavor coconut oil, melted
- 1 tsp garlic powder
- salt and pepper to taste (bonus if you have lemon pepper seasoning)
- salt and pepper to taste
- 1 box of high protein chickpea pasta (or brown rice noodles work, too!)
- 1/2 cooked organic chicken sausage or vegan sausage chopped very small
- 1 cup of cooked broccoli chopped very small

DIRECTIONS

1.Boil water and cook pasta. Once pasta is cooked, drain and set aside.

2. To make the sauce, place butter, garlic and seasonings and broccoli in a rimmed skillet and cook until broccoli is wilted and sausage is softer.

3. Add sauce noodles with the vegetables and heat over medium-low heat.

4. Serve warm with a side of fruit and veggie.

PREP TIME: 10 MINUTES
COOK TIME: 30 MINUTES
TOTAL TIME: 40 MINUTES

VEGAN POTATO FLOUR PIZZA

INGREDIENTS

- 1 cup gluten-free all-purpose flour, plus more as needed (can be made grain-free if using cassava flour or almond flour)
- 2 medium yellow potatoes, peeled and chopped
- 1 tsp garlic powder
- 1 tsp onion powder
- 1/4 cup, plus 2 tbsp arrowroot flour
- 1 tsp sea salt
- 1 tsp baking powder
- 1 tbsp Italian seasoning
- pizza sauce
- 1 package of vegan cheese style shreds
- 1 small handful of spinach

PREP TIME: 10 MINUTES
COOK TIME: 20 MINUTES
TOTAL TIME: 30 MINUTES

DIRECTIONS

1. Preheat your oven to 425°F. Line a baking sheet with parchment or a silicone baking mat and set aside.
2. Place your peeled and sliced potatoes into a pot and cover with cold water. Bring that to a rolling boil and cook until the potatoes are fork tender. Reserve 1/4 cup of the cooking liquid off to the side. Drain the potatoes and place them along with the spices to your food processor and blend until creamy.
3. Whisk the flour, seasonings, and arrowroot powder together. Add to your potato mixture and blend. The dough will be sticky but hold together nicely.
4. Flatten the dough until it looks like pizza crust. Bake for 12-15 minutes or until golden.
5. Remove and top with your pizza sauce, vegan cheese, and vegetables. Cook another 5 minutes or until your cheese is melted and thoroughly cooked through. Slice and serve. Enjoy!

APPLE SLICES AND VEGAN DATE CARAMEL

INGREDIENTS

- 1 green apple, sliced
- 1 serving of vegan date caramel (flip back to this recipe in the Dessert Recipe section!)

DIRECTIONS

1. Slice 1 green apple.
2. Serve with a scoop of date caramel for a classic favorite. Enjoy!

CREAMY VEGAN FUDGESICLES

INGREDIENTS

- 1/2 ripe soft avocado
- 1 1/2 banana
- 2 tbsp maple syrup
- 1 tsp cacao
- 2 tsp cocoa powder
- 1 cup oat milk

DIRECTIONS

1. In a food processor or high-powered blender, blend all ingredients together.
2. Pour contents into silicone popsicle molds.
3. Freeze until solid. Best if frozen overnight.
4. Enjoy immediately!

HOMEADE VEGAN GUMMIES

INGREDIENTS

- 1 cup juice (any juice flavor works, this one is orange juice and lemon juice)
- 1 tbsp maple syrup or sweetener of choice
- 3 tsp agar powder

DIRECTIONS

1. Pour juice into a pot. Add the agar powder and optional sweetener at this time.
2. Turn the burner on high and once the mixture starts bubbling turn to medium and keep stirring for 2-4 minutes until the mixture thickens.
3. Use a dropper or spoon (depending on thickness) into the molds.
4. Place in fridge or freezer for up to 1 hour.

PREP TIME: 10 MINUTES
COOK TIME: 10 MINUTES
TOTAL TIME: 20 MINUTES

SUNBUTTER AND JELLY ENERGY BITES

INGREDIENTS

- 1 cup old fashioned oats
- 2 tbsp sunbutter or nut butter of choice
- 2 tbsp raspberry jam or raspberry puree
- 1 tbsp hemp seeds
- 1 tbsp chia seeds
- 6 tbsp maple syrup, honey, agave, or date syrup
- ½ tsp salt
- 1/2 tsp vanilla extract
- pinch of salt
- optional: 1 scoop vegan vanilla protein powder

DIRECTIONS

1. Place all ingredients in a large mixing bowl.
2. Mix ingredients with hands until evenly mixed. It will be sticky.
3. Roll mixture into balls with hands and place energy balls into a storage container or on a cookie sheet lined with parchment paper.
4. Let cool for 1 hr in fridge and harden before serving. Enjoy!

PREP TIME: 10 MINUTES
COOK TIME: 0 MINUTES
TOTAL TIME: 10 MINUTES

HIPPIE
KIDS
KITCHEN

GO-TO SNACKS, BABY PUREES, WEEKLY MEALS

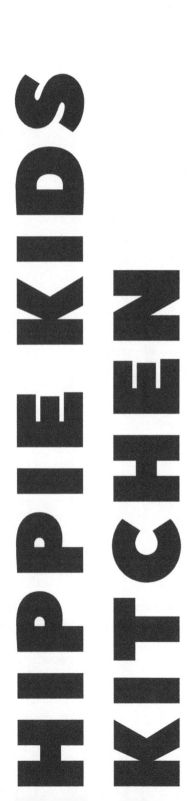

M/W/F

BREAKFAST

Fresh fruit, avocado slices and chocolate chip mu[...] cake OR bowl of gluten-free vegan oats with blueberries and vegan yogurt

LUNCH

Vegan protein smoothie, veggie slices, fresh fruit and avocado toast OR healthy potato flour pizza, fresh fruit, side of veggie

DINNER

Serving of dinner (creamy lemon and broccoli pas[...] fresh fruit and veggie side

T/TH

BREAKFAST

Cold pressed juice, fresh fruit, healthy tot sneaky veggie cookies and vegan yogurt

LUNCH

Double chocolate superfood granola bar, veggie slices, chickpeas, fresh fruit OR vegan fruit smoot[...] vegan buttered lentil pasta with fresh fruit

DINNER

Serving of dinner (vegan shepherds pie), side of veggie, fresh fruit and avocado

HIPPIE KIDS
KITCHEN

SAT

BREAKFAST

Vegan banana pancakes, fresh fruit, veggie sausage OR vegan gluten-free oats with berries and fruit smoothie

LUNCH

Cold-pressed juice, veggie slices, avocado toast, chickpeas and fresh fruit

DINNER

Serving of dinner (vegan spaghetti) with veggie side and fresh fruit

SUN

BREAKFAST

Healthy apple sauce vegan donuts, vegan yogurt and fresh fruit

LUNCH

Vegan protein smoothie, veggie slices, black beans and fresh fruit

DINNER

Serving of dinner (any recipe from Hippie Eats)

GO-TO SNACKS

HIPPIE KIDS KITCHEN

SMOOTHIE WITH VEGAN PROTEIN

COLORFUL SNACK PLATE

VEGAN GRANOLA BARS

HEALTHY TOT SNEAKY VEGGIE /FRUIT COOKIES

APPLE SLICES & DATE CARAMEL

CHOCOLATE CHIP MUG CAKE

BANANA NICE CREAM

HEALTHY ENERGY BITES

FRESH FRUIT AND VEGGIE SLICES

BABY
PUREE
COMBOS

As moms, we know making your own baby food can feel special, healthier and not to mention more affordable. Here are a few simple combinations we loved for our babies.

These combinations are quite simple and nutritious and can be made in a high powered blender or food processor until smooth.

● ●

SWEET POTATO PUREE

Sometimes simple one ingredient purees do the trick. To make thin, you may use breastmilk, formula or filtered water.

SWEET PEA, SPINACH AND PEAR

This combo is sure to please. To make thin, you may use breastmilk, formula or filtered water.

APPLE CAULIFLOWER PUREE

Combine warm steamed apples and cauliflower for a sneaky way to add in some veggies. To make thin, you may use breastmilk, formula or filtered water.

BROCCOLI PEAR APPLE

Steam the fresh or frozen broccoli, peeled pears and apples before adding to the blender.

BLUEBERRY BEET BANANA

We reccomend steaming the beets until soft, then tossing it in the blender with blueberries and bananas.

AVOCADO BANANA

To make avocado puree for a baby, you just need a fresh avocado, a blender, and some lemon juice if you plan to store it for later. This combo is also perfect with banana.

Living Plant- Based

Tips for the whole family

So, you tell your friends, family or pediatrician that you're eating more plant-based. Here are the biggest questions you may hear and here's how we answer to them.

Calcium: There are many plant-based sources of calcium in plants, including certain leafy green vegetables like kale and spinach. Broccoli, tofu, tempeh, hempeh, tahini, almonds, legumes, oranges and seaweed all have great amounts of calcium as well. Typically, plant-based foods are higher in calcium than dairy products.

Protein: This is always a big concern by curious folk, but don't worry. If your kid won't eat meat, don't force it! We see a lot of moms push meat or dairy because they worry about protein. Kids are pretty intuitive, and I've learned to trust that they ultimately know what they need (minus to occasional fit for candy!). For plant-based protein, we incorporate plenty of nuts, seeds, legumes, and a daily vegan protein shake.

Iron: Good plant sources of iron include lentils, chickpeas, beans, tofu, cashew nuts,chia seeds, hemp seeds, pumpkin seeds, kale, dried apricots and raisins. Other sourcesinclude quinoa, pea and cacao.

Fatty Acids: For brain and eye development, it's important to incorporate healthy fats in our kiddos diets. We love adding avocados, hemp seeds, avocado oil, coconut oil, nut butters, seeds, and more.

Vitamin B12: Luckily, this is an easy fix. You can find many kid friendly and adult B12 supplements.

We are not doctors or registered dietitians, so please be sure to check with yours before making any serious changes to your diet first.

Build the best plate

How to add the most nutrition with success

 **Color**

 **1 fruit + 1 veggie**

 **Fiber**

 **Protein + fat**

Good sources of plant-based calcium.

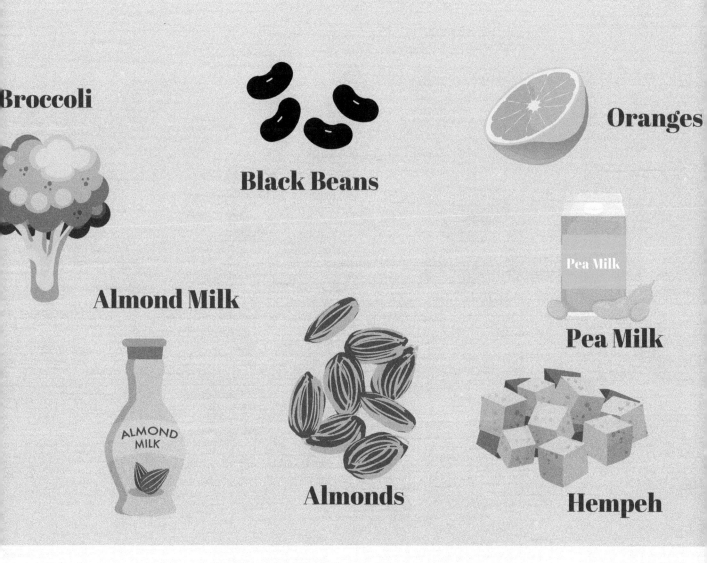

Broccoli

Black Beans

Oranges

Pea Milk

Almond Milk

ALMOND MILK

Almonds

Pea Milk

Hempeh

Good sources of plant-based protein.

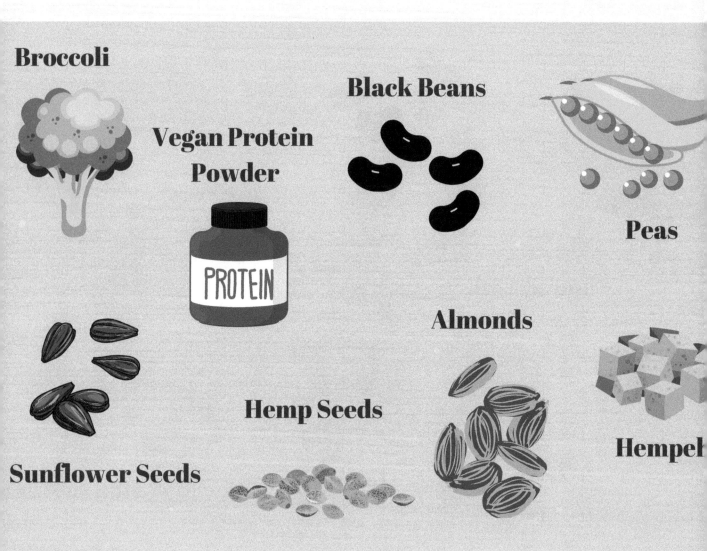

Broccoli

Vegan Protein Powder

Black Beans

Peas

PROTEIN

Almonds

Sunflower Seeds

Hemp Seeds

Hempeh

Good sources of plant-based fats.

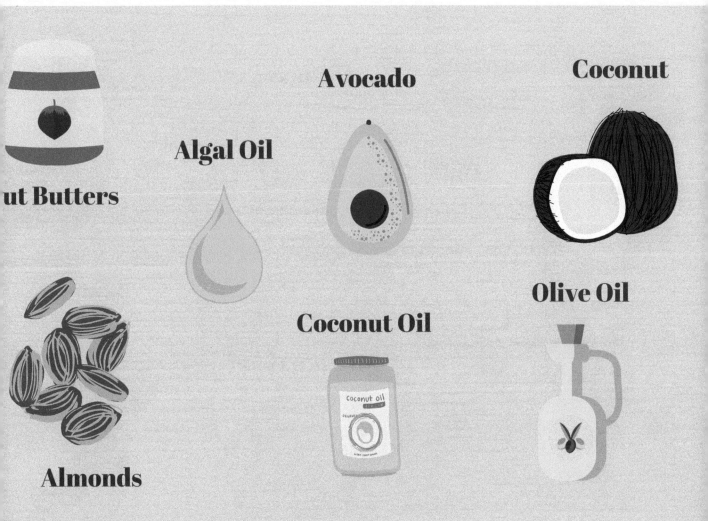

ut Butters

Algal Oil

Avocado

Coconut

Almonds

Coconut Oil

coconut oil

Olive Oil

Good sources of plant-based carbohydrates.

Quinoa

Apples

Oats

Sweet Potatoes

Beans

Bananas

Rice

**"The food you eat
can be either the safest and most
powerful form of medicine or the
slowest form of poison."**

\- Ann Wigmore

"I only feel angry when I see waste. When I see people throwing away things we could use."
—Mother Teresa

BEST OIL CHOICES

- Avocado oil
- Coconut oil
- Walnut oil
- Macadamia nut oil
- Olive oil
- Algal oil
- Hemp oil
- Pumpkin seed oil

BEST OIL-FREE SWAPS
(1:1 REPLACEMENTS)

- Apple sauce
- Banana
- Pumpkin
- Avocado
- Vegan greek yogurt
- Coconut cream
- Squash
- Sweet potato puree

BEST EGG-FREE SWAPS
(RATIOS FOR ONE EGG)

- Apple sauce (1/4 cup)
- Banana (1/2 banana)
- Pumpkin (1/4 cup)
- Avocado (1/4 cup)
- Vegan greek yogurt (1/4 cup)
- Coconut cream (1/4 cup)
- Squash (1/4 cup)
- Flax (flax egg = 1 tbsp ground flax + 3 tbsp water)
- Chia (chia egg = 1 tbsp chia seeds + 1/3 cup water
- Nut butters (3 tbsp)
- Agar agar (1 tbsp + 1 tbsp water)
- Sweet potato puree (1/4 cup)

BEST GF FLOUR CHOICES

- Oat flour
- Almond flour
- Coconut flour
- Rice flour
- Buckwheat flour
- Chickpea flour
- Cassava flour
- Quinoa flour
- Arrowroot
- Sorghum flour
- Amaranth flour

BEST DAIRY-FREE MILK CHOICES

- Almond milk
- Coconut milk
- Oat milk
- Hemp milk
- Pea milk
- Hazelnut milk
- Walnut milk
- Macadamia milk
- Flax milk
- Rice milk
- Cashew milk

BEST DAIRY-FREE
CHEESE CHOICES

- Almond based cheese
- Coconut based cheese
- Cashew based cheese
- Nutritional yeast
- Vegan parmesean
- Vegan cheese singles
- Vegan cheese shreds

BETTER SWEETENER CHOICES

- Coconut sugar
- Maple syrup
- Dates
- Date sugar
- Honey
- Stevia
- Monk fruit
- Lucuma
- Brown rice
  syrup

Eco-
Eats.

LOW-WASTE &
UPCYCLING KITCHEN

WHY LOW WASTE?

The earth is in dire need of our help. We can reduce our carbon footprint by reducing what we consume, elimininating plastic when we can, using resuable straws and containers as well as recycling. Living low waste is easier than it seems. Try swapping throw away plastic straws for either silicone, metal or bamboo resuables. Buy glass containers or repurpose the ones you own.The more we consume, the more waste we create. The most waste we create, the harder it is for planet earth to heal and grow. Currently all waste is headed for landfills that pollute the air and harm wildlife. We care a lot about this planet and those that live on it. Here are some simple low-waste hacks for your kitchen.
Every little bit helps.

1

DITCH THE PLASTIC SHOPPING BAGS; BRING AND REUSE YOUR OWN

It's important to reduce the impact of plastic bags on the environment. Every single-use plastic like water bottles and shopping bags are crowding landfills and endangering wildlife. This small step makes a big difference.

2

REUSE FOOD JARS AND GLASS CONTAINERS

Before tossing your spaghetti jars in the trash, consider reusing them for another purpose, also known as "repurposing." You can use old jars for storage, cups, drinkware and in place of plastic food containers. And hey, we think they are cute, too!

3 REPURPOSE FOOD WASTE

Juice waste can easily be composted; the pulp can be added to granola, thrown int
smoothie, dehydrated to make fruit leather or even dog treats. You can also use veg
peels and onion skins to make veggie broths or compost for your garden.

HINK LIKE A HIPPIE

"e do our best to support brands and
y products that serve and protect
e environment. There are so many
en products and companies these
's, which makes it easier than ever
o make a difference. Check your
nds and products if you aren't sure.
If not, try to find products with
ninmal plastic and lower waste for
planet. And usually, if it's bad for the
lanet, it may also be bad for your
health."- Amber Fokken
& Brittany Bacinski

CPSIA information can be obtained
at www.ICGtesting.com
Printed in the USA
BVHW022116220221
600862BV00023B/356